Table of Contents

To the Teacher

The 10 reproducible activity sheets in this book provide instructional support for the Holt Student World Atlas. Each activity sheet links to one or more specific atlas sections, as indicated on the activity sheet. The first two activities introduce students to the atlas and general map concepts. The remaining activities help students explore the sections of the atlas covering the world, the continents, and the United States.

Each activity sheet provides 10 questions that require students to interpret and use the maps, charts, and graphs in the atlas. An Answer Key is provided for these questions. In addition, the activity sheets for the continents and the United States provide extension activities, which require a more in-depth use of the atlas. Extension activities include both individual and group work, and can be assigned as homework or extra credit.

Holt Student World Atlas

Activity 1
Map Skills

IDENTIFYING MAP TERMS

Refer to the sections "Using This Atlas," "Legend/Projection/Scale," and "Latitude and Longitude" to complete this activity. Use the clues to fill in the letter blanks with the correct terms. Unscramble the boxed letters to find a hidden word.

1. This map item shows what the distance between two points on a map represents.

___ ___ ▢ ___ ___

2. These imaginary lines from a grid over Earth, which enables us to pinpoint the exact location of any spot on Earth.

___ ▢ ___ ___ ___ ___ ___ ___ ; ___ ___ ___ ___ ___ ▢ ___ ___ ___

3. This map item explains what the symbols and patterns on a map represent.

▢ ___ ___ ___ ___ ___

4. These are ways of showing the round Earth on flat maps.

___ ___ ___ ___ ___ ___ ___ ___ ___ ___ ▢

Bonus Hidden Word

___ ___ ___ ___ ___

USING LATITUDE AND LONGITUDE

In each blank, write the city located at the latitude and longitude listed. To find each city, use the political map for the continent in parentheses.

___________________ **5.** 30°N, 90°W (North America)

___________________ **6.** 34°S, 58°W (South America)

___________________ **7.** 60°N, 30°E (Europe)

___________________ **8.** 31°N, 30°E (Africa)

___________________ **9.** 19°N, 73°E (Asia)

___________________ **10.** 31°S, 122°E (Australia and Oceana)

Holt Student World Atlas Activity 2

Using Thematic Maps

IDENTIFYING PURPOSES OF MAPS

Use the section "Different Kinds of Maps" to complete this activity. In the space provided, describe the purpose of each type of map.

1. physical maps:

____

2. political maps:

____

3. thematic, or special purpose, maps

____

IDENTIFYING THEMATIC MAPS

In each space below, write the type of thematic map you would use to answer the question. Choose your answers from the list in the box.

climate	historic route	population density
continental drift	land use	vegetation
gross domestic product	locator	

_____________________ **4.** How is the land in California used?

_____________________ **5.** How crowded is New York City?

_____________________ **6.** What are some of the poorest countries in the world?

_____________________ **7.** How does the climate in Toronto, Canada, differ from that in Miami, Florida?

_____________________ **8.** What route did Christopher Columbus sail to reach the Americas in 1492?

_____________________ **9.** Where are the world's tropical rain forests located?

_____________________ **10.** How do scientists believe Earth's continents have moved over time?

Holt Student World Atlas

Activity 3

The World

EXPLORING THE WORLD

Use the "World" section to complete this activity. Answer the questions in
the spaces provided.

1. Which continents lie entirely north of the equator, and which continents lie entirely
   south of the equator? Which continents cross the equator?

   ____

2. What is the main climate along the equator? at the poles?

   ____

3. Which continent has the world's largest desert?

   ____

4. In 2000, which country had the world's highest population density?

   ____

5. In 2000, which regions of the world had a low life expectancy at birth?

   ____

6. In which part of the world is undernutrition expected to increase in the future?

   ____

7. How do the main religions in North America compare to those in South America?

   ____

8. What regions of the world have the most major manufacturing and trade centers?

   ____

9. Which parts of the world have the highest levels of cell phone use?

   ____

10. How many time zones would you go through if you flew around the world?

   ____

Holt Student World Atlas

Activity 4

North America

EXPLORING THE REGION

Use the "North America" section to complete this activity. Match each description in the left column to the correct term in the right column. Write the term's letter in the space provided.

_____ **1.** The largest country in North America

_____ **2.** The large country located to the south of the United States

_____ **3.** The large mountain range to the west of the Great Plains

_____ **4.** The capital of Canada

_____ **5.** The fairly densely populated country located to the south of Florida

_____ **6.** The climate of much of Canada

_____ **7.** The vegetation of much of Central America, or the area south of Mexico

_____ **8.** The vegetation of the central United States

_____ **9.** The main land use in much of the western United States

_____ **10.** The environmental issue affecting such large cities as Los Angeles, Vancouver, New York City, and Mexico City

a. Poor air quality

b. Ottawa

c. Cuba

d. Livestock ranching

e. Subarctic

f. Tropical seasonal and scrub

g. Tropical rain forest

h. Midlatitude grassland

i. Mexico

j. Canada

k. Rocky Mountains

l. Appalachian Mountains

ACTIVITY

Select a city in North America where you would like to live. Write a journal entry explaining your choice. Your explanation must refer to information from at least three of the maps in the "North America" section. For example, you might say that you would enjoy living in Denver, Colorado, because you like large cities but would also love living near the Rocky Mountains. The highland climate there would be excellent for skiing.

Holt Student World Atlas

Activity 5

The United States

EXPLORING THE REGION

Use the "United States" section to complete this activity. Read each sentence below and fill in the blank with the best choice from the options provided in parentheses.

1. Louisiana is the _______________________. **(Hoosier State/Pelican State)**

2. The _______________________ lies between the Sierra Nevada and the Wasatch Range in the western United States. **(Central Lowland/Great Basin)**

3. The highest point in the United States is _______________________, which is in Alaska. **(Mt. McKinley/Mt. Whitney)**

4. A _______________________ is the boundary or high ground that separates the rivers flowing toward opposite sides of a continent. **(continental divide/fall line)**

5. Many industrial cities developed along the _______________________ between the Coastal Plain and the Piedmont in the eastern United States. **(fall line/fault)**

6. _______________________ is the hottest and driest spot on record in the United States. **(Death Valley/Prospect Creek Camp)**

7. In the United States, _______________________ is the only state in which tropical rain forest occurs. **(Florida/Hawaii)**

8. In the United States, _______________________ is the leading state in vegetable and dairy production. **(California/Wisconsin)**

9. In 2000, the _______________________ was the region of the United States in which the most people lived. **(Northeast/South)**

10. _______________________ is the only country with a higher per capita income than the United States. **(Luxembourg/Switzerland)**

ACTIVITY

Use the information in the "United States" section to create a poster highlighting various facts and features about your state. Consider your state's flag, capital, nickname, major cities, interesting physical features, climate, vegetation, and land use and resources.

Holt Student World Atlas

Activity 6

South America

EXPLORING THE REGION

Use the "South America" section to complete this activity. Read each of the following descriptions, and write the country, region, or physical feature that is "speaking" in the space provided.

_______________________ **1.** "I am South America's largest country." Who am I?

_______________________ **2.** "We are the two countries with the highest GDP per capita in South America." Who are we?

_______________________ **3.** "I am a long mountain range that runs along the west coast of South America." Who am I?

_______________________ **4.** "I am the longest river in South America." Who am I?

_______________________ **5.** "We are the only two landlocked countries in South America?" Who are we?

_______________________ **6.** "I am the South American country with the highest energy use per person." Who am I?

_______________________ **7.** "I am a South American country that lists uranium among its mineral resources." Who am I?

_______________________ **8.** "I am the large basin at the heart of South America's tropical rain forest." Who am I?

_______________________ **9.** "I am the mountainous land region in eastern Brazil." Who am I?

_______________________ **10.** "I am a French territory located in northeast South America." Who am I?

ACTIVITY

Write a one-paragraph description of one of the following city regions: Manaus, Brazil; São Paulo, Brazil; Lima, Peru; or Santiago, Chile. Consider population and major cities, land use and resources, climate, precipitation, vegetation, environmental issues, and any interesting features. Refer to the "South America" section for information.

EXPLORING THE REGION

Use the "Europe" section to complete this activity. The sentences below
are **FALSE**. Make them **TRUE** by replacing the underlined words.

1. The largest country in Europe is <u>France</u>, and its capital is <u>Paris</u>.

____

2. The <u>North</u> Sea is both the largest lake and the <u>highest</u> point in Europe.

____

3. The <u>Balkan Peninsula</u> is a vast plain stretching across much of Northern Europe.

____

4. The highest point in Europe is located in the <u>Alps</u>.

____

5. <u>Italy</u> and the United Kingdom are part of the British Isles.

____

6. The most densely populated area of Europe is the <u>northeast section</u>.

____

7. The <u>Mediterranean Sea</u> provides a rich source of oil and gas for Europe.

____

8. Europe's poorest area, based on per capita GDP, is the <u>northeast</u>.

____

9. Most of Europe has either a marine or <u>ice cap</u> climate.

____

10. Much of Europe has poor air quality and is affected by <u>desertification</u>.

____

ACTIVITY

Write three questions that can be answered using information in the
"Europe" section. Then form a group with two to four other students.
Compete to see who can answer each group member's questions first.

Holt Student World Atlas

Activity 8

Africa

EXPLORING THE REGION

Use the "Africa" section to complete this activity. Match each description in the left column to the correct term in the right column. Write the term's letter in the space provided.

_______ **1.** Largest country in Africa	**a.** Sahel
_______ **2.** Large island off the coast of southeast Africa	**b.** Rabat
_______ **3.** Capital of Morocco	**c.** Marine
_______ **4.** Large basin in South-Central Africa	**d.** Algeria
_______ **5.** Land region directly south of the Sahara	**e.** Sudan
_______ **6.** Large desert in northern Africa	**f.** Sahara
_______ **7.** Wealthiest country in West-Central Africa, based on per capita GDP	**g.** Desertification
	h. Wadi Halfa
_______ **8.** Climate in the country of Lesotho	**i.** Gabon
_______ **9.** A leading environmental issue in Africa	**j.** Madagascar
_______ **10.** Location with the lowest average annual precipitation in Africa	**k.** Acid rain
	l. Congo Basin

ACTIVITY

Use the "Africa" section to find an interesting feature of Africa. Then create a print advertisement for a travel agency promoting a trip to Africa that is centered around the interesting feature you selected. You might use an encyclopedia or other resources in your classroom or school library to find additional information about the feature.

Holt Student World Atlas

Activity 9

Asia

EXPLORING THE REGION

Use the "Asia" section to complete this activity. Read each sentence below
and fill in the blank with the best choice from the options provided in
parentheses.

1. The large country that extends into both Europe and Asia is

_______________________. **(China/Russia)**

2. The country of Saudi Arabia is located on the _______________________.
(Arabian Peninsula/Deccan Plateau)

3. Turkey lies between the Mediterranean Sea and the _______________________.
(Black Sea/Red Sea)

4. The capital of Iran is _______________________. **(Baghdad/Tehran)**

5. The most densely populated regions of Asia are the South and the

_______________________. **(East/West)**

6. China has a lower per capita GDP than _______________________. **(India/Japan)**

7. _______________________ is the main land use in Asia. **(Agriculture/Forestry)**

8. Vast oil fields are located in _______________________ Asia.
(Northeast/Southwest)

9. Much of Southeast Asia has a _______________________ climate.
(subarctic/tropical wet)

10. The main vegetation on the Arabian Peninsula is _______________________.
(coniferous forest/desert)

ACTIVITY

Imagine that you are taking a car trip from Delhi, India, to Beijing, China.
Write a letter to a friend describing the climate and vegetation along the
way. You might also mention any interesting sights you see. Refer to the
"Asia" section for information.

Holt Student World Atlas

Activity 10

Australia/Oceania

EXPLORING THE REGION

Use the "Australia/Oceania" section to complete this activity. Use the description in the right column to unscramble the term to the left. Write the correct term in the space provided.

YENYSD

1. ___________________ Largest city in Australia/Oceania

WNE LEADANZ

2. ___________________ Country located across the Tasman Sea from Australia

RISCIOMANE

3. ___________________ Name of the area where the Caroline Islands are located

UAPPA

4. ___________________ First word in the name of the second-most populous country in Australia/Oceania

TILASARUA

5. ___________________ Country in this region that produces diamonds

NAIRME

6. ___________________ Main climate in New Zealand

RIDA

7. ___________________ Climate of central Australia

ALNERCT

8. ___________________ Region of Australia that gets the least precipitation

SETOFR

9. ___________________ Last word in the name of the type of vegetation found on the island of Tasmania

VIYEDRISIBTO

10. ___________________ Loss of this is a leading environmental problem in Australia and New Zealand

ACTIVITY

Imagine that you are going to open a business in Australia. Write a letter to a fictional bank asking for a loan to help fund your new business. Your letter should explain what type of business you plan to start, what you will produce, and where you plan to settle in Australia. Refer to the Australia/Oceania Land Use and Resources map for information.

ACTIVITY 1

1. scale
2. latitude; longitude
3. legend
4. projections

Bonus Hidden Word: atlas

5. New Orleans, Louisiana
6. Buenos Aires, Argentina
7. St. Petersburg, Russia
8. Alexandria, Egypt
9. Mumbai, India
10. Kalgoorlie, Australia

ACTIVITY 2

1. physical maps—to show the physical or natural world
2. political maps—to show political divisions and features on Earth
3. thematic, or special purpose, maps—to show information about a specific subject or closely related subjects
4. land use
5. population density
6. gross domestic product
7. climate
8. historic route
9. vegetation
10. continental drift

ACTIVITY 3

1. north—North America, Europe, Asia; south—Australia, Antarctica; cross—South America, Africa
2. equator—tropical wet; poles—ice cap
3. Africa
4. India
5. sub-Saharan Africa and Egypt, central and eastern South America (Brazil, Bolivia, Guyana), the Caucasus (Georgia and Azerbaijan), parts of Southwest and Southeast Asia (Yemen, from Kazakhstan to Cambodia, Papua New Guinea)
6. sub-Saharan Africa
7. Both are mainly Christian, but North America is largely Protestant, while South America is largely Roman Catholic. Both continents have pockets of local religions and Islam, but Judaism is only significant in North America.

8. eastern North America, Europe, eastern Asia
9. much of Europe, Australia, New Zealand, Japan, South Korea, Taiwan, Israel
10. 24

ACTIVITY 4

1. j: Canada
2. i: Mexico
3. k: Rocky Mountains
4. b: Ottawa
5. c: Cuba
6. e: Subarctic
7. f: Tropical seasonal and scrub
8. h: Midlatitude grassland
9. d: Livestock ranching
10. a: Poor air quality

ACTIVITY 5

1. Pelican State
2. Great Basin
3. Mt. McKinley
4. continental divide
5. fall line
6. Death Valley
7. Hawaii
8. California
9. South
10. Luxembourg

ACTIVITY 6

1. Brazil
2. Argentina, Chile
3. Andes
4. Amazon River
5. Bolivia, Paraguay
6. Suriname
7. Argentina
8. Amazon Basin
9. Brazilian Highlands
10. French Guina

ACTIVITY 7

1. Russia, Moscow
2. Caspian, lowest
3. Northern European Plain
4. Caucasus Mountains
5. Ireland
6. northwest
7. North Sea
8. southeast
9. humid continental
10. acid rain

ACTIVITY 8

1. e: Sudan
2. j: Madagascar
3. b: Rabat
4. l: Congo Basin
5. a: Sahel
6. f: Sahara
7. i: Gabon
8. c: Marine
9. g: Desertification
10. h: Wadi Halfa

ACTIVITY 9

1. Russia
2. Arabian Peninsula
3. Black Sea
4. Tehran
5. East
6. Japan
7. Agriculture
8. Southwest
9. tropical wet
10. desert

ACTIVITY 10

1. Sydney
2. New Zealand
3. Micronesia
4. Papua
5. Australia
6. marine
7. arid
8. central
9. forest
10. biodiversity

Student World Atlas
Activities with Answer Key

HOLT, RINEHART AND WINSTON
A Harcourt Education Company

Student
World
Atlas

Activities with Answer Key

ISBN 0-03-093420-6

8 9 10 11 12 13   0956   12 11 10 09